DEAD!

CONTENTS

Watts Books
London • New York • Sydney

DYING

All living things die. It's the one thing we can all be certain of. In the past, dying was a lot more unpleasant than it is today. The average age of people when they died in the Stone Age was less than eighteen years. The main causes of death were disease and violence.

Fortunately, in western countries nowadays, most people die peacefully in old age. There are even special nursing homes called hospices to care for people who are dying of incurable illnesses.

The image of the Grim Reaper is often associated with death.

On the island of Samoa sick old chiefs used to ask to be buried alive.

Some species of mayfly live for only a few hours after they emerge from their larvae.

The lifespan of the elephant is roughly the same as that of humans - about seventy years.

Different cultures have different ways of dying. Old people of the Omaha tribe of Native Americans would stay behind when the rest of their family group moved camp. They were left enough food for just a few days.

Some species of birds live to a great age. Cocky, a male sulphur-crested cockatoo, died in London in 1982 aged over 80.

The most famous hospice in the world was founded by a nun called Mother Teresa. Her hospice was founded to look after people dying on the streets of Calcutta.

Er... I can't think of anything! Err...

Buddhists believe that their dying thoughts will have an important influence on their next life.

Some Hindus try to say the word 'om' with their last breath. They believe that this may help them to escape the cycle of reincarnation.

Trees live a lot longer than animals. The oldest tree is thought to be 'General Sherman', a giant sequoia tree in California about 3,000 years old.

DEAD BODIES

After death the muscles of the body relax. Relaxation starts in the jaw which falls open, and then spreads out through the body. At the same time, because the blood has stopped circulating, it sinks and causes stains on the skin which look like bruises. About six hours later, rigor mortis sets in. This is a stiffening of the muscles which again starts at the jaw and spreads out through the body. Rigor mortis normally lasts about thirty hours, then relaxation of the muscles spreads out once more from the jaw. Rigor mortis may set in immediately if death occurs at a time of stress. This is why suicides may be found gripping the revolver or sword with which they killed themselves.

William the Conqueror died after a fall from his horse in 1087. His stomach swelled and burst open before he could be buried. There was a terrible stink during his funeral service at Caen cathedral.

In a warm climate, putrefaction, or rotting, starts after a few days. First, a greenish tinge appears around the stomach and spreads outwards. Then, the stomach swells up with gases like a balloon, and can burst open. Finally, liquefaction (going runny) starts at the eyeballs and finishes with the stomach, liver and womb (in women). Bones do not putrefy.

In subzero temperatures, bodies do not decompose (rot).

A 45 year old woman died standing upright in a timber yard in the town of Wahncau in Germany. Rigor mortis had set in at the moment of death.

eek!

If death occurs during exercise, rigor mortis can set in immediately. During the charge of the Light Brigade in 1854, an officer's head was blown from his body. The body galloped on upright and stiff in the saddle with his sword still held high.

Home guide to head shrinking

Remove the head from the body.

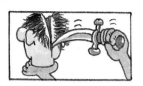

Make a cut from the back of the neck to the crown of the head.

Remove the skin from the skull and discard the skull.

Sew the eyelids together. Sew the lips together.

EMBALMING

Nowadays many bodies are embalmed. It makes them look peaceful and it stops them smelling before the funeral.

The body is first placed on a trolley and washed in soap and water. Then embalming fluid is pumped into it through an opening in a vein, normally near the armpit. Embalming fluid is a mixture of preservative (usually formaldehyde), disinfectant and colouring. As the fluid spreads through the veins, the body regains a healthy pink colour. Then, after four to six pints have been pumped in, the blood is drained out of the body through another opened vein into a vacuum container on the floor.

The process of replacing the blood with embalming fluid takes about three-quarters of an hour. Afterwards, a surgical instrument called a trocar is plunged into the abdomen and scooped around until all the soft tissue has been removed. Cavity fluid is then pumped in to fill up the empty space.

In order to give the face a calm expression, the jaw is sewn tight with thread through the inside of the lips. This is a picture of Rosalia Lombardo of Palermo, Sicily, who died in 1920 aged two. Rosalia's face is especially peaceful and well-preserved by injections given to her body immediately after death.

Boil the scalp and face for two hours.

Place hot stones in the scalp to shrink the skin.

Smoke overnight.

Hang above the fireplace.

Bodies are sometimes embalmed naturally. Tollund Man, who was probably a fertility sacrifice to the goddess Ertha around 500 BC, was preserved intact in a peat bog until discovered in 1950 at Tollund in Denmark. His features are so well-preserved that even the stubble of his beard is completely visible.

A preserved head from ancient Peru. A cactus spine has been inserted through the lips.

Tourists queue to see Lenin's body in his open tomb outside the walls of the Kremlin, Moscow.

Perhaps the most famous body to be embalmed this century is that of Lenin, the leader of the Russian revolution. The body is kept in a temperature-controlled mausoleum in Red Square, Moscow, and is visited by thousands of tourists every year. Every eighteen months the body is taken out and soaked in a special preservative fluid.

In ancient Babylon, bodies were sometimes embalmed in honey. It is said that the body of Alexander the Great was preserved like this.

BURIAL

If dead bodies are left lying around, they quickly rot and become a danger to health. Throughout history the commonest way to dispose of the dead has been to bury them underground. In some of the earliest graves of prehistoric Europe, stones were often laid on top of a body. It was thought that this would stop the dead from returning to haunt the living. For the same reason the feet were often tied together. Red ochre might be sprinkled on a body to represent the blood and strength it would need in an afterlife.

In modern graves there should be a depth of about six feet between the coffin lid and the surface. At the end of the funeral a few handfuls of earth are scattered on the coffin. The rest of the earth is replaced using a mechanical digger after the mourners have left.

If a body is to be buried at sea, holes must be drilled into the coffin so that water can get in to make the coffin sink.

The Vikings sometimes buried their dead under the thresholds of their houses. This was because they thought that the souls of the dead could defend their houses against evil spirits.

Other ways to dispose of bodies

The Aborigines of Australia left dead bodies in trees.

Hurry up –
He's going off!

In the Solomon Islands the dead were laid out on a reef for the sharks to eat.

Tibetans have no respect for dead bodies once the soul has left them, and will even hack them to pieces for the birds to eat.

In China it is considered very important to bury a corpse in the right spot. An astrological chart with an inset compass is often used to determine the exact position and alignment for the body.

Suicide is a sin in the Christian religion. People who committed suicide were not allowed burial in Christian graveyards and were often buried at crossroads.

Fear of burial alive was widespread in the nineteenth century. A special apparatus was invented by Count Karnice-Karnicki which involved a vertical tube running from the coffin to a box above ground level. A glass sphere resting on the chest of the corpse was connected via the tube to a flag, a light and a loud bell. Any small movement of the chest would activate the mechanism.

High in the mountains of the Hindu Kush, bodies are buried upright in the snow.

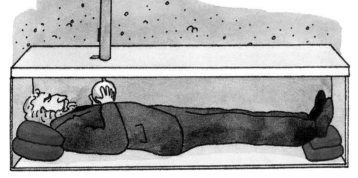

Muslims like to be buried on the same day as they die. The body should be placed on its right side, facing Mecca. On the other hand, Buddhists like to be buried facing north.

Some Inuits cover the corpse with a small igloo. Because of the cold the body will remain for ever unless it is eaten by polar bears.

The Parsees of Bombay used to leave their dead on the top of tall towers to be eaten by vultures. The vultures devour the corpses to the bone within five minutes.

You're a genius Sydney!

The Taj Mahal is one of the seven wonders of the modern world. It was built by the Mogul Emperor Shah-Jehan for his favourite wife Arjamund Begum. Arjamund died in 1631. Work on the mausoleum started in 1632.

MEMORIALS

The earliest Christian tombstones were simple stone slabs known as ledgers. Later the ledgers were sometimes raised up on legs to form table tombs. Chest tombs were table tombs with the sides enclosed.

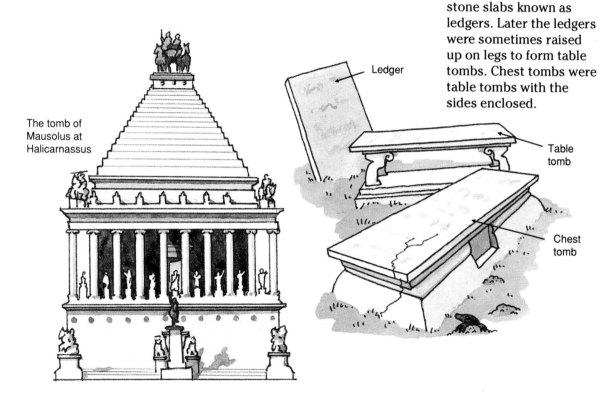

The tomb of Mausolus at Halicarnassus

Ledger

Table tomb

Chest tomb

It is human vanity to hope that we shall be remembered after we die. In many historic cultures, more money has been spent on memorials for the dead than on homes for the living. The richer and more powerful the dead person, the bigger the memorial. Mausolus was a Persian King in what is now south-western Turkey. His huge, white marble tomb at Halicarnassus was one of the Seven Wonders of the Ancient World. It was built by his wife Artemisia (who was also his sister). Artemisia mixed his ashes in wine and drank the mixture. She later joined him in their mausoleum.

It took 20,000 men working for 22 years to build the Taj Mahal.

The Emperor wanted his building to be unique. When it was finished, the hands of the craftsmen were chopped off so that they couldn't build another one like it.

Elvis Presley is buried at his home called Gracelands, in Memphis, USA, which is now an Elvis museum as well as his mausoleum.

The burial mounds of native North American Indians were sometimes built in the shapes of birds and animals. Some of these mounds were built as early as 700 BC.

Great Serpent Mound, Ohio

The tomb built for the Chinese Emperor Qin Shihuangdi was said to contain rivers of mercury. Crossbows were set to fire at grave robbers automatically. The workmen who built the tomb were walled up inside to stop them giving away the secrets of its construction.

The great pyramids are among the largest structures ever built. The pyramid of Cheops is made up of 2,500,000 blocks of stone of an average weight of 2.5 tonnes. Its height is over 140 metres and 100,000 workers took more than 20 years to build it.

The tomb of Karl Marx, the founder of communism, is in Highgate Cemetery in London.

GRAVE GOODS

The custom of burying things with the dead is at least 60,000 years old. The rich and powerful were buried with treasure, and even with their servants. Ordinary people were buried with food and drink and sometimes cups and tools. Things may have been buried with dead bodies because it was believed that they would be useful in the after-life. Much of what we know about ancient people has been learned from studying their grave goods.

The tomb of the Qin Emperor of China contained an army of life-sized clay soldiers and the bodies of all his concubines who were killed specially for his burial.

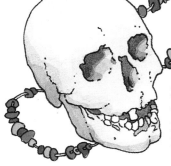

Some Bronze Age people only buried a dead person's skull with a few possessions.

In ancient China, jaw bones of pigs were buried with the dead.

The Egyptian pyramids were like palaces stuffed with treasures. The tomb of Tutankhamun contained the largest hoard of ancient golden artefacts ever found.

Neanderthal graves 60,000 years old have been found containing the remains of flowers.

The Egyptian queen Her-Neith was buried with her favourite dog.

A thirteenth century Maharajah of Jaipur was buried with his favourite elephant.

In India, a Mogul prince was buried with his barber.

The burial ship of a Saxon king dating from AD 650 was found at Sutton Hoo. It contained some of the richest treasures ever found in England.

The Adena tribe of Ohio placed clay tobacco pipes in graves, in case the dead should wish to smoke.

In the Middle Ages, consecrated bread was buried in the grave, so that the dead could offer it to God. Priests were buried with a cross and a cup as well as the bread.

The royal tombs of ancient Sumeria had running water so that the dead could drink.

Nowadays, if children die, their favourite toys may be buried with them.

Among other things, the ancient Celts would put games in the grave so that the dead would have something to amuse themselves with in the next world.

CREMATION

In AD 789, Emperor Charlemagne decreed death for anyone practising cremation. Cremation was considered unchristian because it was thought that a burned body could not be resurrected at the Last Judgement.

The first cremations in the USA were carried out in Washington in 1876, in the private crematorium of a doctor, Julius Lemogne. In Britain, the first legal cremation took place in 1883 when Dr William Price, an 83 year old Welsh druidic priest, cremated his five month old baby, whom he had named Jesus Christ Price.

Modern crematoriums reduce a body to ashes in about one and a half hours. The newest models working at temperatures up to 1,200 degrees centigrade are even quicker. Wood ash from the coffin is light, and goes up the chimney together with any water vapour, leaving the bones and the ashes of the body behind. Any metal, for instance gold from teeth, is collected from the ashes. Finally, the bone fragments are crushed to a fine powder in a special machine. The final residue per adult weighs about three kilograms. This is collected into a tin can with a screw top, ready to be emptied into an urn or to be scattered.

An early crematorium

The Beaker people who lived in Europe around 4,000 years ago used to collect the ashes of their dead in beakers or decorated pots.

Suttee was a cruel tradition common in India until banned by the British in 1829. Widows were expected to burn alive with their dead husbands, sometimes cradling their husband's head on their laps and lighting the fire themselves. In 1780, when Rajah Ajit Singh was cremated, sixty-four of his wives were burned alive with him.

Gypsy kings and queens are burned in their caravans.

Os resectum is a mixture of burial and cremation. A finger is cut off and buried, while the rest of the body is burned. The buried finger is the seed for the new body which will be resurrected on judgement day.

Viking leaders were placed in their favourite long boat, which was then set alight and pushed out to sea.

The poet Percy Bysshe Shelley drowned off the coast of Italy in 1822. His body was burned on an open fire on the beach. Wine, incense and oil were thrown on to the flames. Trelawney, his friend, plucked the heart from the fire, badly burning his own hand. The heart was returned to England in a box.

Nowadays, cremation is forbidden for orthodox Jews, Parsees, Muslims and Greek Orthodox Christians. Hindus always cremate their dead. The eldest son lights the funeral pyre.

Cryonics is a method of freeze drying bodies in the hope that they can be thawed out and brought back to life in the future. People ask for this treatment because they believe that a cure for the cause of their death may be discovered in the future.

After death the body must be connected immediately to a heart-lung machine and packed in water ice.

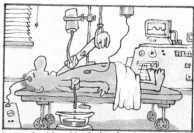

Later the blood is drained out of the body, and replaced with preservative fluid.

DEEP FROZEN FUTURE

The population of the world is now 5,000 million people and it's still growing. About 5 million tonnes of dead bodies have to be disposed of every year. The problems of disposal are going to increase in the future.

Cryonics poses many problems. In particular, would future generations want to revive thousands of frozen bodies?

Millions of bodies were mummified in ancient Egypt. If it were possible for us to revive them, would we want all those ancient Egyptians to look after?

In the USA today some people pay up to $150,000 to be mummified after death using techniques based on those of the ancient Egyptians.

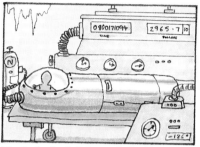

Finally the body is frozen in liquid nitrogen. Keeping it frozen is very expensive.

It's unlikely that cryonics is effective. To really work, bodies should be frozen before they die.

Are you dead yet?

Nearly!

The first dead body to be permanently frozen was James Bedford, a Californian teacher of psychology, in 1967.

Quick drying may be used in future to preserve bodies for later revival. In 1954 the body of a ten year old Inca prince was discovered in a cave on a mountain near Santiago, Chile. The child had died 500 years before but the body had been very well preserved in the cold, dry air.

The frozen bodies of mammoths have been found in the ice of Siberia. Their meat could still be eaten after thousands of years. In the future people may consider it wasteful to burn or bury 5 million tonnes of nutritious dead bodies every year. They could be frozen and eaten instead!

INDEX

First published in 1993 by
Watts Books
96 Leonard Street
London EC2A 4RH

Paperback edition 1994

10 9 8 7 6 5 4 3 2 1

Franklin Watts Australia
14 Mars Road
Lane Cove
NSW 2060

© 1993 Lazy Summer Books Ltd
Illustrated by Lazy Summer Books Ltd

UK ISBN 0 7496 1186 3 (hardback)
UK ISBN 0 7496 1596 6 (paperback)

A CIP catalogue record for this book is
available from the British Library
Dewey Decimal Classification: 393

Printed in Belgium